D1641605

To a very special person

Always in my thoughts

_____

_____

_____

Honoring the Earth

I walk in beauty upon Mother Earth,
rejoicing in the abundance of her gifts.

I walk in beauty upon Mother Earth,
inspired by her power and mystery.

I walk in beauty upon Mother Earth,
celebrating the splendor of her dance.

I walk in beauty upon Mother Earth,
honoring all that is sacred,
and living in the spirit of her song.

Turtle Island
by Adrian Pushetonequa
(Sac/Fox/Mesquakie)
oil on canvas, 1970

Turtle songs echo through sandstone canyons, fresh blooms of cactus and great seas.
Those songs remember and connect us to the center.

Untitled
by Brenda Ho[…]
(Miwok)
oil on canvas
ca. 1966

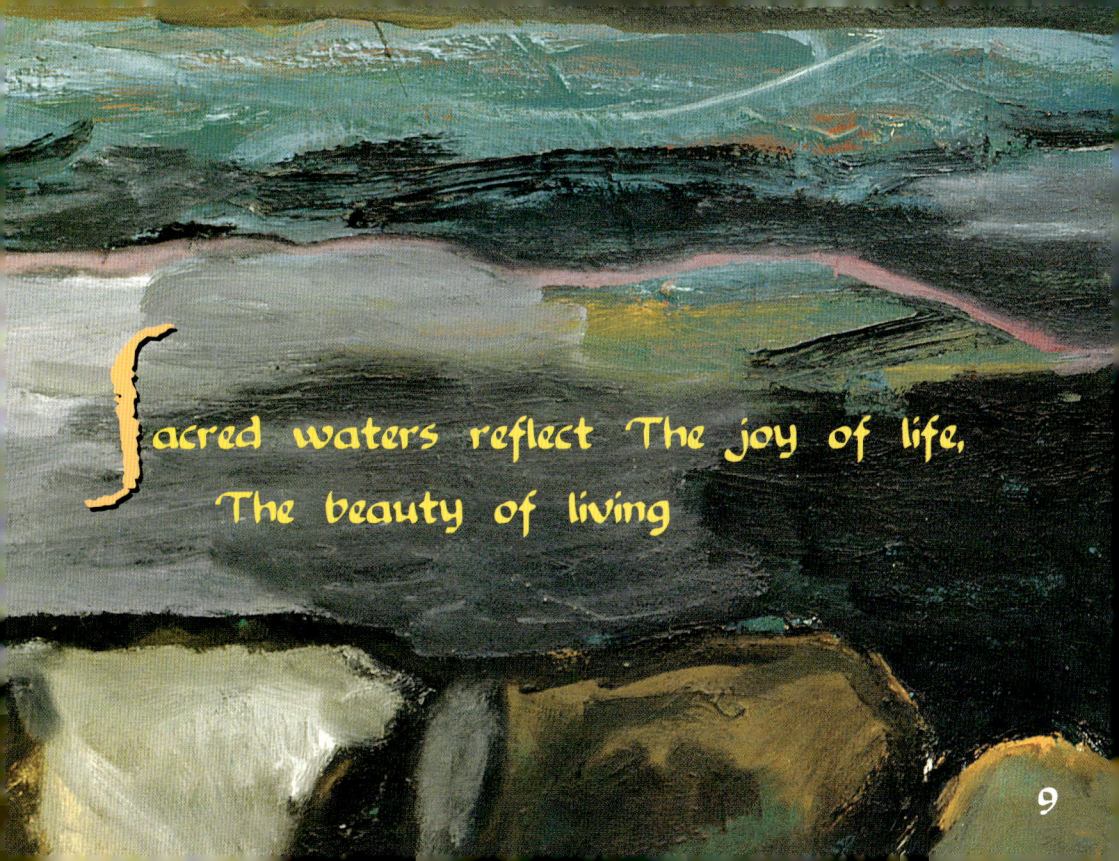

Sacred waters reflect The joy of life,
The beauty of living

Untitled
by Carl Cannc
(Oneida)
acrylic on can
ca. 1970

I see my mother standing
in morning light.
How beautiful she looks
at day break.

Untitled
by Sakahaftewa Ishii (Hopi)
acrylic on canvas,
1980

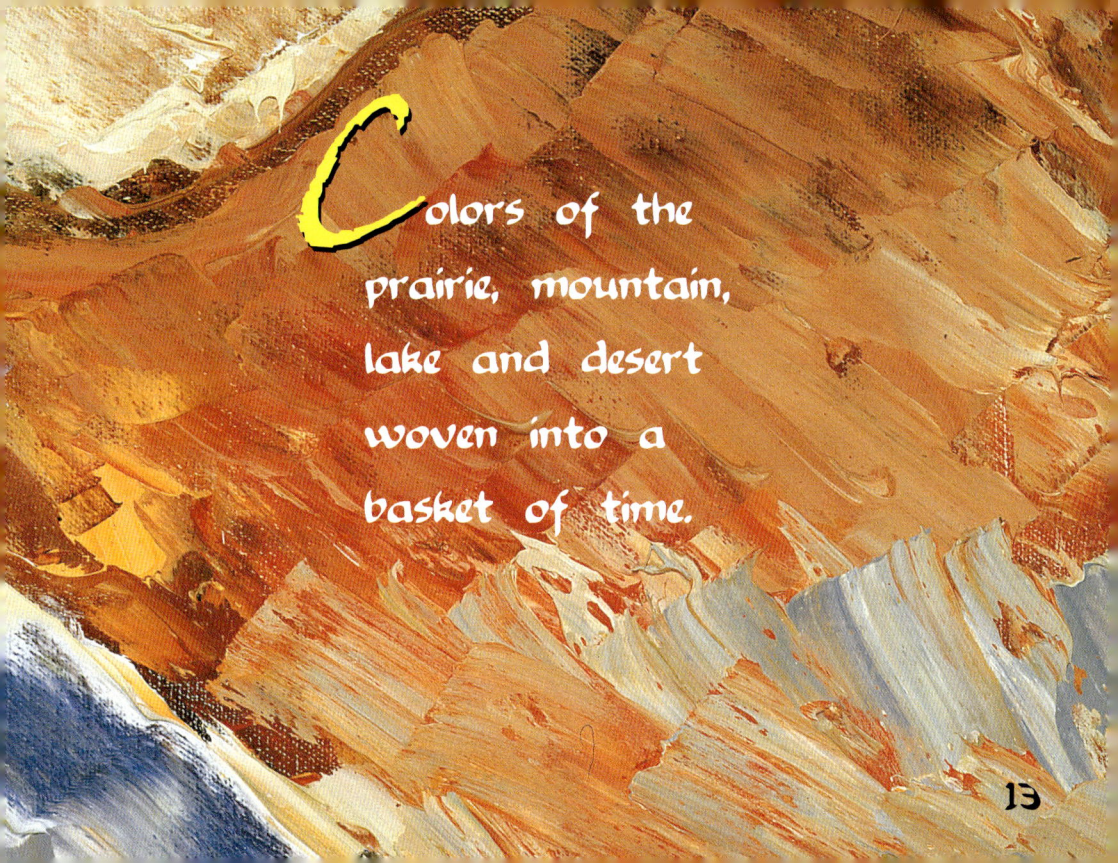

Colors of the prairie, mountain, lake and desert woven into a basket of time.

by Grey Cohoe (Navajo)
oil on canvas, ca. 1966

Quiet rainfall brings calm to the heart, peace to the spirit.

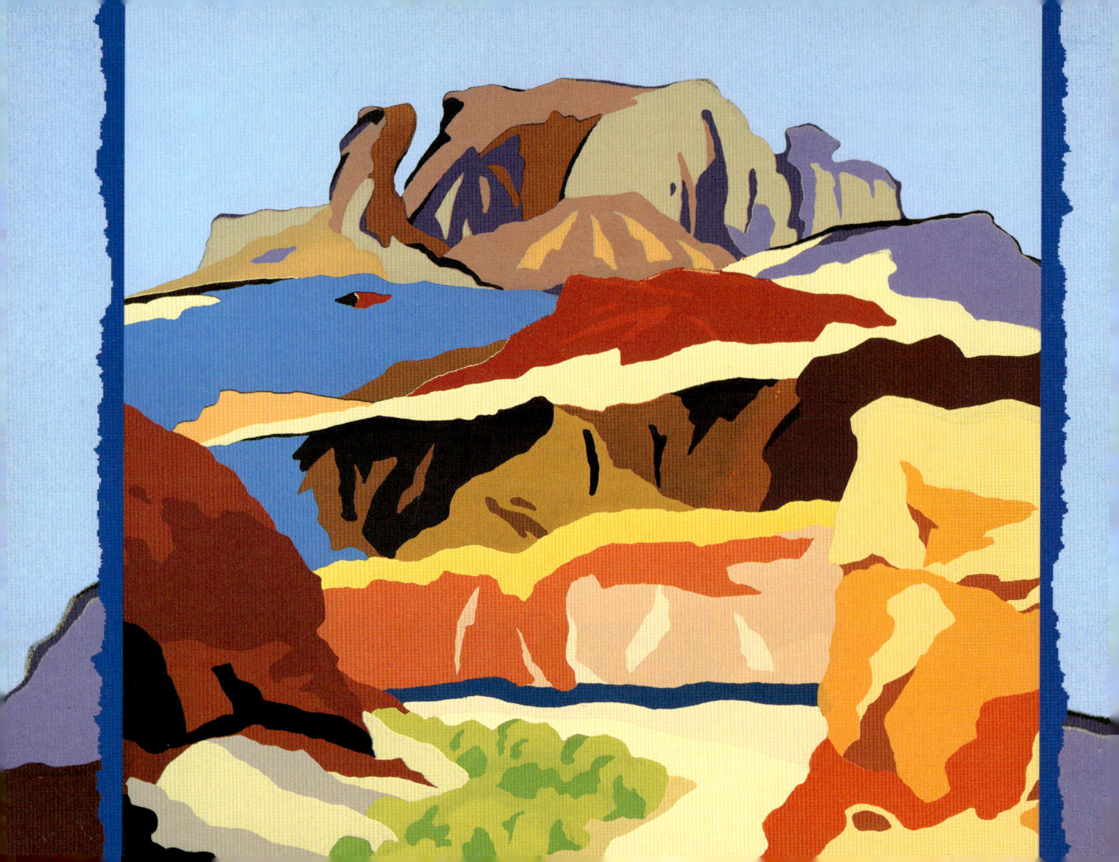

Day passes through ancient cedar rings and damp white clouds.

The Shadows
Norman Akers (Osage)
screen, ca. 1985

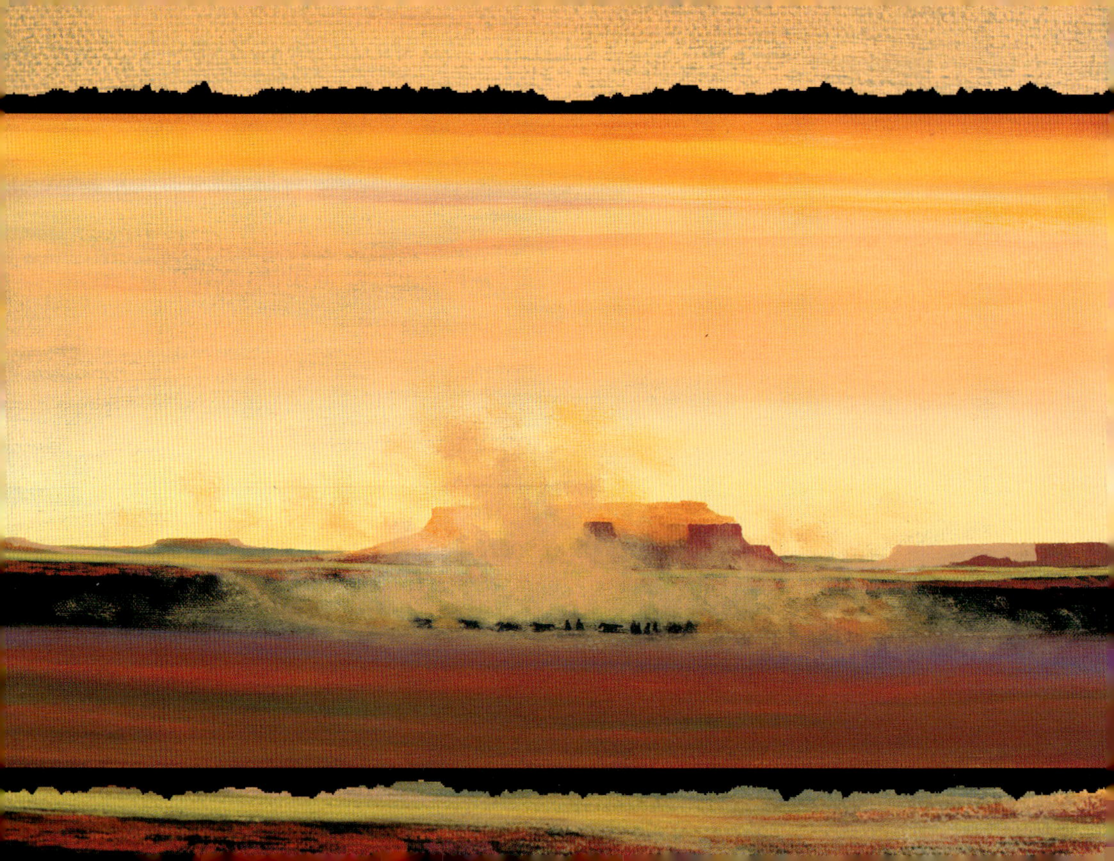

Sky and Earth join to await dawn's greeting. Morning is alive with silence.

Untitled Landscape
by Anthony W. Suina (Cochiti Pueblo)
Oil on canvas, ca. 1972

by Carlos Fr
(Athebascan)
oil on canvas
ca. 1968

First light awakens
Mother Earth
Gently giving rise
to the day.

Untitled
by Luke Simon (Micmac)
acrylic on canvas,
1988

Cloud shadows fall and rise beside me.
I am surrounded by beauty.

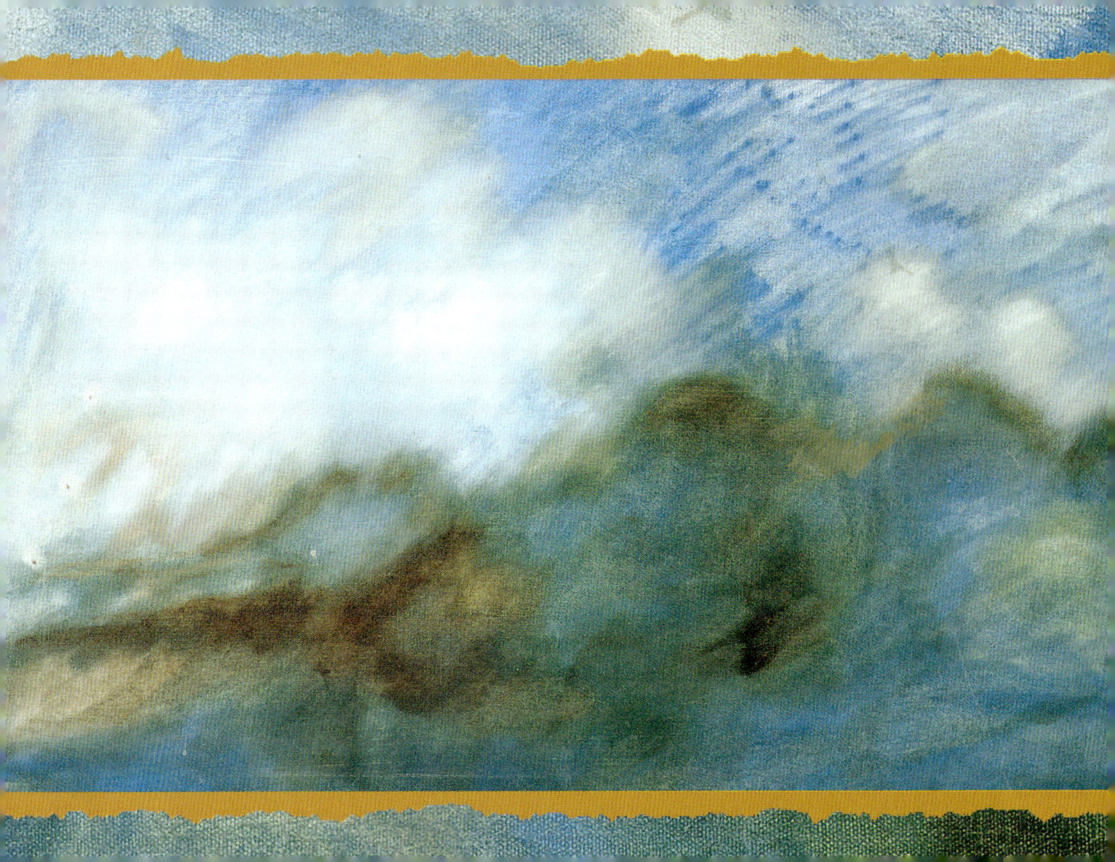

Dawn fades into day. Clouds form and smooth ribbons of air remain, blue and light.

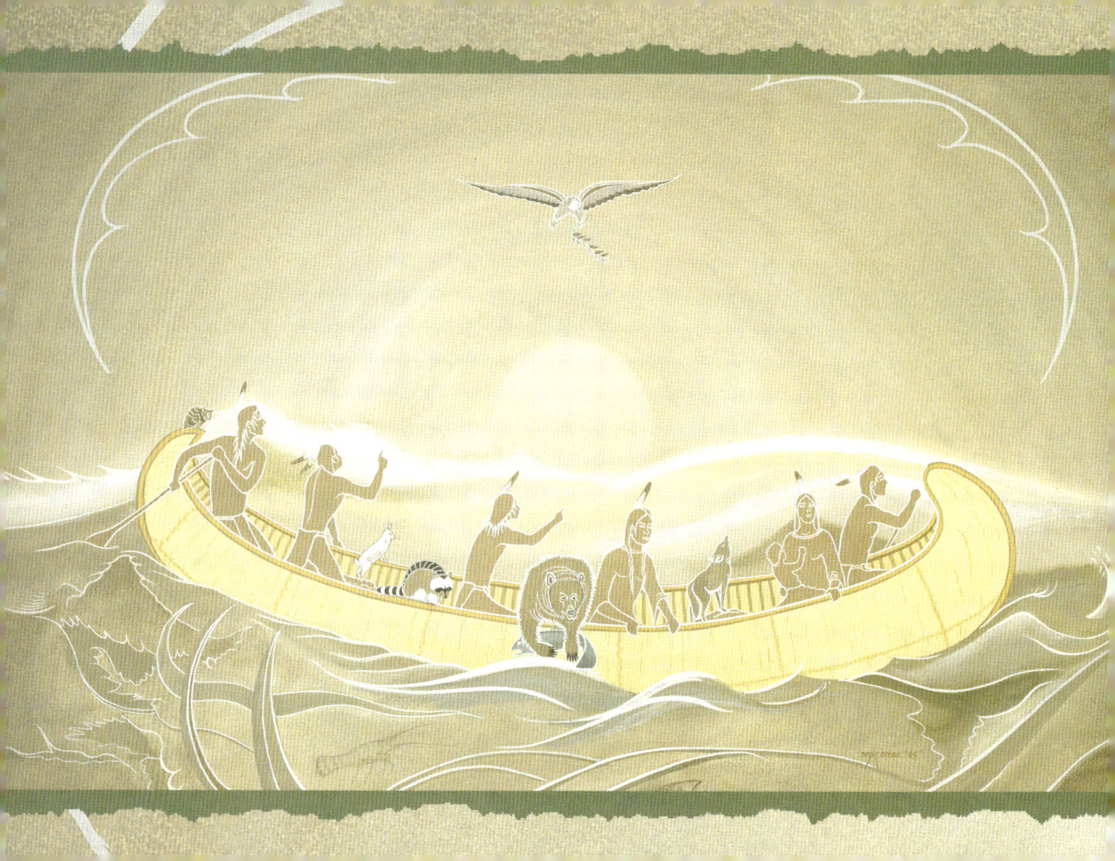

Creation breathes life
Into those birthed
of ice and water.

Creation Story
Soloman McCombs (Creek)
tempera, 1965

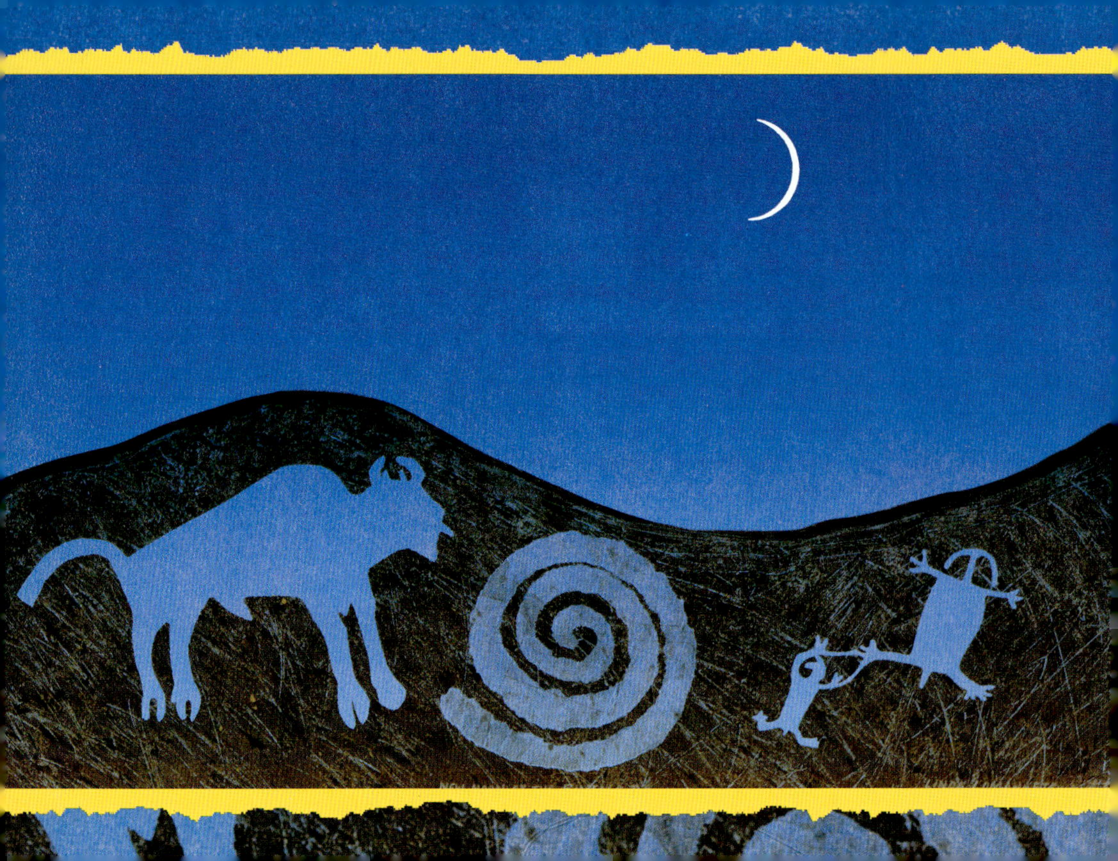

Night beings travel roads of blue and indigo light.

New Moon of the Buffalo
Linda Lomahaftewa
Hopi/Choctaw
monotype, 1994

My thoughts on what is...

Enjoy these simple moments...

Institute of American Indian Arts

The Institute of American Indian Arts (IAIA) is pleased to share 13 of the nearly 6,500 objects of art in the National Collection of Contemporary Indian Art. The images in this writing journal are a modest indication of the talent and creativity of the 3,700 students from nearly all of the 558 federally recognized tribes who attended our college in the 20th century. These works represent the largest and most diverse collection of contemporary American Indian art in the world.

The publication of this journal is one facet of the IAIA initiative to provide American Indian and Alaska Native students with access to opportunities through higher education, time for students to study and immerse themselves in the unique cultural and artistic traditions of American Indian and Alaskan Native peoples. All of the proceeds from the sale of this collection support student education and a long-term goal to expand our academic program.

Thank you for helping IAIA continue its "tradition of creativity."

For more information on the IAIA, or to pledge your support please contact:
The Institute of American Indian Arts
83 Avan Nu Po Road Santa Fe, NM 87505   1-800-804-6423   Web Site: www.iaiancad.org
Visit our on-line gift shop for additional works of art. www.iaiagiftshop.com

Poetry: RoseMary Diaz
Tewa (Santa Clara Pueblo)
Design/Production:
Creative Works

TURTLE ISLAND PUBLISHING

Printed in China

Poetry by RoseMary Diaz

RoseMary Diaz has been writing poetry for more than twenty-five years, and received her first of many literary awards in 1974 while attending the Santa Clara Pueblo Day School in northern New Mexico.

RoseMary's poetry is heavily influenced by the ancient teachings of her Pueblo heritage, and by many of the traditional poetic forms of China and Japan. Her voice is one of truth and compassion, and speaks through the poetic images of universal spirituality and wisdom.